Walking in God's Path

By Judy Ball

Dedication

When I was thirteen years old my mother was very ill with cancer. My little brother had polio and our family was covered by prayer from our local church and friends. During that time we had a cousin living with us who worked with my father until he had the money to go to seminary. He was our Mary Poppins. (He helped keep our family together by praying and playing with us). Every afternoon when he came home from work he would take his Bible and walk into the woods and stay for an hour or two. On several occasions I followed him and saw him sitting by a tree reading the Bible and talking out loud to God.

After he left I began to do the same thing. I read the words in red and prayed and listened and the Lord began to answer all my prayers. It was my joy to bring light and happiness that I found at the moss bed to my family and my friends. All my life I have listened for words from the Father for guidance and words of encouragement from Him to give to others.

I hope these words from the Father will bless you and bring you light, hope and joy in this dark world.

I dedicate this book to my beloved husband, Jerry, of 50 years.

Conversations with God

Day 1: Conversation with God

"My beloved, I am the one who loves you with an everlasting love and I know your quest this year is to love me more and more. As you start on the home stretch of your life you will be younger and younger as you eat my word and drink my blood. I love you. I love you. I am so happy that you have chosen love over hate and patience and kindness over impatience and your flesh. I love you. I am he, the Lord."

Thank you so much for this time with my children. I love you, Lord. I put the children under the blood of Jesus. I leave them there knowing that all the words, all the light, and all the prayers are hovering over them, looking for a place to enter that will break open the life in them and the hope of glory. I love you, Lord. I love you, Lord.

"This year you will see thousands saved and you will preach the gospel and all the mind games the enemy tries to play with you will be gone as you continually put your brain on the altar and say that you have the mind of Christ; say you have his wisdom and he cast down all imaginations and thoughts that are not of me. I love you, daughter. Go home with a streak of glory and go forward and not backward. Pray for the children of the world. Read all of Colossians. On the way home, digest it."

Day 2: Conversation with God

Lord, I want you to touch me radically. I want to be totally transformed by your Holy Spirit and have your life in me and to know the knowledge of your word. I want to walk as one with my husband in the Holy Spirit and I want to be what you created me to be. I ask to be recreated in Christ and to do those good things you ordained me to do from before the foundation of the world. I want to be strong all day and refreshed in the Spirit.

Lord, will you help me to love my children perfectly?

Lord, teach me about the King of Babylon – Baal. Jesus, you are King and your kingdom rules in my life. You are in me, the hope of glory.

Isaiah 2, Psalm 8, Ephesians 2, Jeremiah 4, Galatians 2:10, Micah 4.

"I am sending the fire off the alter right now. I love you. Amen."

"Right this minute trust me to separate the dross from your spirit, soul and body. It is "not by might or by power, but by my Spirit, says the Lord." Each day starts with the beauty of the glory of the Lord. My word says: "the earth showeth forth his handy work day unto day and night unto night." Each day brings beauty in family, friends and the body of Christ. Then the wages of sin bring forth the vile all around us. We are tempted to take the vile out by might and power, but I tell you that it is not by might nor by power, but by my Spirit. Read the words to Jeremiah in 15:18, 19."

Day 4: Conversation with God

I trust you now, this minute, by your power and your Spirit to remove the dross from my spirit and body and mind leaving only the beauty of life in all that happens each day. Not by might and not by power but by your Spirit. Each day brings the glory of your handiwork, but plastered on its horizon and nearby are vile wages of sin that can cause me to believe that by might and power I can separate the precious from the vile. It is not by my might and not my power, but by yours, Lord.

Day 5: Conversation with God

Dear Lord, what do I do now?

"My beloved, this time you are crucified and I will give you love and power and a sound mind. I will make it possible for you to be at peace all the time and I will direct your path. All is well. All is well. Give me all the glory and cast down all ugly thoughts. Cast down all fears, cast down all things that do not pertain to godliness. All is well. Rejoice, as I am in charge of all of this. I will oversee this, as I have all other things in your life that you release to me. "Now, it shall come to pass in the latter days that the mountain of the lord will say to the nations to go up to the house of the God of Jacob and hear the word of the Lord from Jerusalem."

*"***Arise and thresh, oh, daughter of Zion. The word says my house shall be established upon the mountain and exalted above the hills. I will teach you my ways and you shall walk in my path."**

Micah 4, Isaiah 2, Psalm 8

Day 6: Conversation with God

"My beloved, today all malice ceases in you and you will not say bad things about anyone, even if it is true. From this day forward--just like I revealed to you the truth about many things and you never went back—well, this is that day. Your mouth has spoken bad things about your brothers and sisters and has caused you to age. Now I have, as you have repented, washed every word that has proceeded out of your mouth that was not of me to be disintegrated in the fire of the Holy Spirit and you will supernaturally be renewed: your skin, your bowels, your bones, and your belly. This is the secret of love and life and eternal power to change things through the love of Jesus and his blood; it makes the work on the cross full of beauty and life and redemption."

"I love you, my dear one. Today is a day of freedom and you will rejoice and be full of my vigor and joy. I Love you, Your Father."

Day 7: Conversation with God

"This day I am going to use you to lift the dying and help those who are weak. Get dressed and pack a lunch. Take a piece of pie and be overjoyed that your loved one is healed in spirit, soul and body. Send your grandchildren home with joy and life and truth."

I love you Jesus and Father.

Day 8: Conversation with God

"Lay your idols down. Lay down your family, your marriage, Ignite Ivy, the Israel trips, and your listening ability. Giving, give, give and give more. Lay your strength down and swap it for my strength. Lay your thoughts down and swap them for my thoughts."

Thank you for restoring a relationship. Lord, speak to me about other relationships that need restoration. I love you, Lord. Peace, peace, joy, joy; now my body, by your power, will pour out all poisons. I thank you, Lord. I thank you, Lord.

"**My beloved daughter, don't let this be a distraction. Trust me all the way. I am crushing pride and emotions and he will be the body of Christ that he wants to be. Leave everything to me. Peace, be still.**"

Day 10: Conversation with God

"My beloved daughter, love and love more. Give and give more."

Lord what do I do now?

"Praise me, praise me, and praise me."

Am I supposed to go tomorrow in the name of Jesus?

"Yes, and I am sending angelic beings to accompany you and to stand with you. Be of good cheer. I have overcome the world and I have destroyed the works of the enemy by faith in my blood. Walk in peace and absolute health. I am with you. I will shower you with blessings while you are gone; blessings of my life and fellowship of my life. Everyday your daughters are coming face to face with me and their children also, and the fear of the Lord and the goodness of God in you bring them to repentance."

Day 11: Conversation with God

Lord, I have done what you said. I see them coming down the drive in the van. What do I do now?

"Call today and ask them to come. I will go ahead of you and cause her to long for home and for the comfort of her mother's arms and her father's blessing. I will dissolve the jealousy that has caused division in this family. Rejoice, as I have colored the black with beautiful colors on my water and light. They were there, but were hidden in the darkness. Now my light is bringing forth the colors and my water of my word is sealing the beauty of my holiness. Rejoice in me always. I love you."

Psalm 2 and 15 and Philippians 4

All is well. He preserved the colors of my spirit, soul and body with His blood, and the colors are written in love and His blood branded me with fire.

Day 12: Conversation with God

"My beloved, today you saw in Ephesians 2 that I recreate in Christ Jesus my called ones to do the good works that I created them to do from the foundation of the earth."

But, Jesus has been removed and there is an intellectual pursuit to see where the leadership is. They are searching a new learning of the minds of men and the counsel of men to find their own way rather than being born again by the Spirit. They deny your good works that you, the Lord, created to do day by day by entering the secret place and listening and forgiving and being forgiven so that the road blocks are removed. They do not know that they can be free with the help of angels, the empowerment of the Holy Spirit, the love of God, and the freedom to do the pure, true and indestructible works of God that bear fruit and are eternal.

"I love you. You are whole and healed. Receive it now; pull down manifestations."

Day 13: Conversation with God

"My beloved, I love you and I am going to lift you up out of this right now. I seal your words of blessings on family right now. I seal the blessings on the women with the blood and the anointing oil of my Glory."

Why am I going?

"I have appointed you to reign over the United States of America and you will have dominion over the devil and over those who have volunteered to get America praying. I am putting my power in your lungs and I am lifting you above this storm."

"This will be the most powerful meeting that this prayer team has ever had absent from the flesh, filled with my fire and power to stand in each state and gather the army of believers who are ready to be crucified and resurrected with me. I am building an army filled with myself and I rule and reign over America."

"Your family is like the little seeds you planted in the dirt. They are putting roots down as they seek me in the darkness, and the light is shining on the roots in the darkness and recreating them in Christ Jesus"

Day 14: Conversation with God

"My beloved daughter, rest assured that I arranged for you to go on this trip today. I have called you. Remember the river boat. Don't expect anyone but I, your Father who made you, to understand. You understand that it is I, who speaks and will speak when I call you up. I block every sprit of jealousy and every spirit of hindrance. You will pray when I call you, and as you walk to the podium the fire from off my altar will fall on you more powerfully than you have ever experienced and all eyes will turn to me, the intercessor, my son Jesus, and the earth will touch heaven and activate the heavenly host that will travel to Israel and to all the world. The manifest presence of my Son will be felt and all demons that would come against you will fall. Love and honor and be full of joy. I am with you and I am sending you with my Spirit without measure. All is well."

Day 15: Conversation with God

"My beloved daughter, there is a noose that is waiting to hang you, but I have delivered you from the fowler and your family--if you do as I say. Love, forgive, intercede with faith and love my word. But do not get your eyes off of the epic battle of the ages that I have called you to be in. I will perfect that which concerns you in my own way. See that you love and care by my Spirit as you do for Israel, my beloved. Prepare yourself with fasting and prayer and I will show you what to do. Today I will once again fill you with my love, power and a sound mind. I love you. I love your daughters and their families. I will keep them in perfect peace when their minds are stayed on me. Israel is a shining light to the nations because all the nations now have my Son and the remnant is praying for Israel. America is a super power and thousands are praying in their cell groups and in mass. I have heard the prayers of my people who are praying and I am smiling and my hand is moving. Listen and obey me and I will send them with a myriad of angels going before and after. That is my promise to you. You will find the fire is consuming all whom I have chosen to be on this trip. Lay each of your family members on the altar and let me provide a lamb, Jesus, for their deliverance from death. Believe. Believe! I love you."

Day 16: Conversation with God

"My beloved daughter, I am the "I AM" and I have called you into the glorious kingdom of my dear Son to rule and reign with him on earth as it is in heaven. Now I want you to know that you too have the power to talk to the wind and the rain and to the principalities and the power of the demonic realm. Speak to the clouds again in the faith of Jesus and rejoice in me that I am the Lord that sends the rain on your garden and you rejoice bringing in the sheaves. When the harvest of souls begins, the same tiredness comes and soon the value of the crop is lost in the blessing in the physical strain of the work. Let rejoicing always be on your lips, bringing in the sheaves. You are ready to see the greatest harvest, both in Israel and in America, before I bring you home to be ever with me in Heaven."

Day 17: Conversation with God

"My beloved, I am the God of all the earth: fear not. I will keep this team as the apple of my eye. I know the motive of each heart is to be my voice and my body, and to affirm my truth to the people of Israel and to the principalities and powers."

"I will keep each one and there will be no sickness, no accidents and no fear. No plans of the enemy to prosper. They will have favor in finances, in health, in peace, and in dying to self. The mindsets that are not mine are in progress of being transformed by the renewing of my word. As they press into me to be cleansed and filled with only Jesus in them, the hope of Glory, all of the things that can trip them up will be dissolved in my incredible love and power. As they thank me for their life, my appreciation for them to be one in me will form a weapon of my glory, and light in a dark land where the pit of hell has come against my city and my appointed land from the beginning of time."

"I will bless each of you. Just die to self and live in my word and don't be offended by anything that happens, but praise me for your plane, for your room, for your food, for the long days, for the bus driver, for the guide, for the leaders. I have appointed you. Just keep your eyes on me and move by my Spirit, as the wings of the cherubim move together without any break."

"Thank you. I love you, and I bless you and your families and your ministries. You will return with revelation and truth and power of the Holy Ghost."

Day 18: Conversation with God

Lord, there are rumors of wars and there are earthquakes in diverse places. What shall the righteous do?

"My child, my word stands. I stand as sovereign Ruler of the universe with righteousness, peace and joy in the Holy Ghost that I sent to all the earth through my Son. Jesus' birth, death, and resurrection made it possible for me to pour out my Holy Spirit on all flesh. My Holy Spirit is here, there and everywhere and you can have as much of the Holy Spirit as you want if you ask Jesus to pour it out on you, or actually manifest it to you, in you and around you. "

"The Holy Spirit is my creative Spirit that made all things out of things that were not made, through my Son, Jesus, on the earth and the heavens. The earth is full of the knowledge of the Glory of the Lord. How can good and evil occupy at the same time? It depends on what spirit speaks to the subatomic particles in the air. Quantum physics has found that the electron that goes around the orbit of the atom responds differently to people, positive to positive speech and negative to negative speech. Jesus said speak to the mountain and it shall be removed by my faith. "

You, Lord said life and death are in the power of the tongue. You spoke and created the earth from words. We speak and our words release the power of the light and glory of God or the darkness and death of the spirit of the devil that resides in the earth because of sin.

"My grace is still on the earth. If all of my life and Spirit were to be removed, evil will destroy everything. The army that believes in Jesus is the salt of the world and the light that dispels darkness."

But the spirit of evil has been released disguised as good. There are those on earth in mass who believe they can destroy the earth with bombs. But you say your kingdom is righteousness, peace and joy in the Holy Ghost and that your kingdom creates and does not destroy.

The good news is that our God reigns and he reigns in goodness and mercy through us all our days and even death cannot separate us from his goodness and mercy and His eternal kingdom. We dwell in the kingdom of God on earth as it is in heaven because Jesus lives in us and He is our resurrection and life. We occupy his kingdom on this earth with the power of the Holy Spirit and his goodness until he comes back or we go to meet him.

God, keep us all and raise up a righteous army that will enforce the law of the Lord that is perfect and converts the soul; a righteous army who has the kingdom of God within them that has no end and all power over the power of the enemy, in the name of Jesus. Give us the unction of the Holy Spirit to speak and declare the words of life and light that destroys the works of the enemy.

Day 19: Conversation with God

"You are going to have more this year than before. It is the set time to favor Zion. I will continue to give Breaker of Dawn favor and finances. Your family has been totally released to me. Now I will convict all sin, of the blessings you have been and are to them and they will cherish you. Watch and see and just realize this is my doing when it happens, not theirs or yours."

"You are my princess and my breath and I am continuing to open doors that you walk through that will bring honor to me. I love you. This morning at church you will have much honor and favor and will be a blessing."

"Be still and know that I am your God. I will keep you. I will promote you to be able to daily spread my love and light to all who come near you. I will place you in places where tornadoes of my love and oceans of my power will turn the tide. Those who have come against you will wake up and fear me and welcome me. They that are the enemies will hate you more, but my wall will protect you my feathers will insulate you."

Day 20: Conversation with God

"My beloved, I will keep you in the palm of my hand. I will deliver your family all the days of their life. The words they have spoken against you will melt like ice. You need to come to me and believe I hear you. The Ignite Ivy group is chosen by me. I will keep them as the apple of my eye. You will continue to speak into their lives. I will gather more and more and more."

Lord, speak to me about this trip.

"The prayers of the people were upon you and today after you read my word I want you to write a report that I will put into your heart."

Lord, I feel lost. I feel the hurt and anger. I feel the silence of unspoken words.

Father, unless you build a house it will not stand. What should I read today?

"I want you to read Psalm 10 starting with 19-29 and then five Proverbs starting with 10-15; then John.

Day 21: Conversation with God

"My beloved daughter, why are you so distressed and why do you fear? I am with you and I will finish what I have started. Be at peace now and breathe my breath of life. Read Psalm 1 and 10 and read Acts 2 and 3. Peace, be with you. My peace will keep you now.

Day 22: Conversation with God

"My child, I have coached you this morning and I seal this session with my blood and my Spirit. Love is the answer. Don't ask questions. Just be and then come home and continue to write and think about Ignite Ivy League. I love you. I keep you now in a hive, in a cocoon of my love, letting you develop into the beauty of my holiness. The blood of Jesus seals this place and keeps you in joy and love. If darkness tries to come into you just close your eyes and say "the blood of Jesus" and be still, and I will brush you off and heal you and strengthen you for the battle. And when it is finished you can spread your wings in strength and fly and the beauty of my holiness will be upon you."

Day 23: Conversation with God

"You are my beloved child. Don't fret or worry about what I have started. I will finish. Just keep pressing in and this conference will light a fire that will start a revival in the Northeast fueled by millions of prayers for the Ivy League schools. I am the Lord who made you. I love you so much. All is well.

"I am smoothing the wrinkles out of this family. I am taking what has been put in a trash heap and laughed over and celebrated as a victory for defeat and I am washing you in my precious Son's blood and pouring my live and my power and my mind into you that will propel this family one by one into the glory. The fullness of time has come for this family. You will rejoice."

I love you, Father. We will feel strong today and all the residue that the enemy has put into us will disappear.

Day 24: Conversation with God

"My beloved, you learned this weekend to separate the precious from the vile. I am precious. No accounts. No accounts. The pure and holy come from the flesh washed in the blood of the Lamb. The pure and holy is the voice of God resurrected in the flesh. The pure and holy is the whole body washed in the blood of Jesus; the pure and holy is righteousness and peace and joy in the Holy Ghost. I am the I AM. I go with you in all circumstances. All is well."

"Today my Spirit of light and joy and peace will evade River Life. A centrifuge of my glory is there and the angels have rushed in from heaven to minister through the blood of Jesus. The pure and the holy are there. You are free. No guilt. No guilt. Release. Release. Keep contending for peace and joy and righteousness. Release the Holy Spirit and wash in the blood. I am the I AM.

Read: Isaiah 10, Mark 5, Psalm 2, Psalm 45, Revelations 2, Micah 4."

Day 25: Conversation with God

"My beloved, just obey me day by day. Know that I will unfold my plans secretly and orderly so that they will not be more than you can do. Rejoice in the fact that your friends are coming today. Rejoice and relax in me. I will direct what you do today. I have covered you with my wings and I keep you in the secret place of the Most High. You, my daughter, will have grids of prayer. Just as was prophesied. I love you; just obey daily."

But what about her, Lord?

"Take your hands off of her. She belongs to me. I am redirecting her life. Don't look at her as a failure or a sinner, but as a beautiful queen who is coming forth in royal beauty and truth. Keep praying the prayer of love and acceptance and speak well of her. Let go of her children and my children and love those I send to you."

Okay, Lord, I will take my hands off of her, her children and her husband. I know they all love you, Lord. You are redirecting all of our lives. I see her as a beautiful queen who is coming forth in royal beauty and truth.

Day 26: Conversation with God

Lord, I repent of my prayerlessness. I repent for not engaging in the fire of your Holy Spirit on the altar more and staying before you until I break through. I ask you to let me have a constant prayer meeting with the saints until I come home to ever pray before the throne and worship you saying, "Holy, holy is the Lord God Almighty who is, who was, and who is to come."

Lord, I thank you so much for my husband and for this time for us. I ask you to interfere with our plans and our life and fill us with the fire of your Holy Spirit and put us where we can do the most devastation to darkness with the light and the glory of Jesus in us, the hope of glory.

Lord, defend Israel with the blood of Jesus. Protect and encourage the believers in Israel who have put down tent pegs for your kingdom and who lay down their life everyday so that your word will manifest. May all of Israel be saved.

Bring your life on every campus in America. Deliver this generation from the worship of Baal and cause them to become the bride of Christ so your joy may be full.

In your presence give us ideas- not flesh ideas, but sovereign ideas that will bring sovereign moves of God. Lord, I ask for youth and strength and power and purity and glory and transformation of our life to your life.

Thank you for Jesus and for revealing Him to us as Savior, Deliverer, Redeemer, Healer and Salvation. We so love you, Father. Thank you. We give you all honor, all praise, and glory forever. Amen

Day 27: Conversation with God

"My beloved daughter, I am the one who loves you and guides you into all truth. I will give you more and more peace and more and more ability to write my words and hear from heaven and speak with authority and gather those who will go together in faith. I love you. Let me transform you. Let me guide you step by step. I will guide you thought by thought and you will obey minute by minute in my peace. You are in the kingdom of Heaven. I will speak through you from heaven down. I love you. Be at peace. I will send those to you whom I want you to know. Trust."

Day 28: Conversation with God

"My beloved, I don't want you to trust one man. Remember man is fallible, and so are you outside of my constant love and attention. Lay your life on the throne again this morning and crucify yourself with Christ. I am crucified with Christ, nevertheless I live, yet not I , but Christ lives in me and the life which I now live in the flesh I live by the faith of the Son of God who loved me, and gave himself for me. I do not frustrate the grace of God. For if righteousness came by the law, then Christ is dead in vain.

What do you require of me, Lord? What do you want me to do?

"Continue to stand in the gap and plug into my love and pour it on them when you do. Read Mark 4, Psalm 4, Revelations 4, Proverbs 4. I will put a wall of fire around you and the glory in the midst of you."

Day 29: Conversation with God

"I have not forsaken you, neither have I abandoned you. You just bow and listen and choose to keep your mind, your soul, your physical body filled with my Spirit and my manna from heaven, which is love. Remember nothing satisfies but my love. All other things are tainted. I love you."

Lord, what about the Washington trip?

"I have a secret place; a place hidden that will cause you to abide and pray. I am faithful. I will keep you. I am cleansing you. Receive me, the hope of glory into your heart, your brain, and your nerves. I am your hope of Glory. I am with you."

Day 30: Conversation with God

"My beloved daughter, I am the I AM. I AM has come. You are my beloved child. I love you with a great love. Today, be careful what you say. Just relax and keep me before your eyes. Have confidence that I will blow out through you the glory smoke from heaven. Just wash in the blood of my Son and bow before me and I will blow my love, my light and my Spirit through you. I love you."

Words from God to this Young Generation

Day 1: Words from God to this young generation

"My child, life right now at times seems like a blurry snow storm where you cannot find your way. If you will be still and listen and look, you will see a small light in the darkness and you will hear a warm word in your ears. This is the way. Walk ye in it."

Day 2: Words from God to this young generation

"I am the I AM. Faint not. Arise and be filled with my spirit. Let go of all your fears and confess them to me as sin. Be still and repent of them because they are like a python squeezing life out of you. My Spirit has not given the spirit of fear but of love and power and a sound mind. Any fear must be repented of and be put under the blood. You are mine. I will keep you through this storm. You cannot see. That is alright. I know and I am a rewarder of them that diligently seek me. I am peace in the storm. I am life among the dead. Keep your eyes on me and stir up the gift in you of my life."

Day 3: Words from God to this young generation

"My children, I love you with an everlasting love and I have put in you the keys of the kingdom to bind and loose on earth what is in heaven. I have given you the secret that you can live by, "Christ in you, the hope of Glory."

"Now I am answering the desire of your heart that I put there because you asked me and that is to use the creative spirit, my Spirit, to bring truth and light to millions. I will give you the desires of your heart because they are pure and holy and you have given your all to me; all the joy and all the sorrow. I love you and I am the wind beneath your sail. Rejoice, as all is well. Let the joy of the Lord bring you great strength and let the peace give you freedom to live in fullness and think my thoughts and create my life on earth as in heaven. All is well. Rejoice."

Day 4: Words from God to this young generation

"My beloved children of faith, love, courage and determination of the Holy Spirit, you have been marked by me. I have placed you, all of your life, near living water because you hunger and thirst after righteousness and truth. I have led you through rugged mountains and deep valleys."

"Fear not."

"There is no valley too deep or a mountain too high, no pain too unbearable that is beyond my touch, my love, and my way."

"I am the way, the truth and the life. I am all you need."

"You will find me in quiet moments when you enter into my presence by the powerful blood of the Lamb. You will find me in my word. I am the Word of Life."

"You will find me in the face of the needy when you see my love transform them into the vessel I made for them, a vessel of hope in a hopeless situation."

"I am the light in the darkest places. I have designed you to carry my light and my love. You choose each day, light over darkness, and forgiveness over strife and love over hate."

"I will hold your hand. I have planned much joy for you as you continue to keep your eyes stayed on me and walk the walk, not knowing where the path leads, but trusting me because you know my faithfulness in the walk behind you. Rejoice in me always."

Day 5: Words from God for this young generation

"My beloved child, you are my pioneer woman. Years ago when a woman found a husband that was a pioneer, she left her family never to see them again. They did not have phones, e-mail, texting, planes or cars. They had children who worshipped God and lived by His grace."

"Follow the Holy Spirit in all you do for your time on earth. Stay close to me when you are lonely, afraid or when life does not make sense. You have the secret: you have me and you have been my beloved child since birth. I revealed myself to you when you were months old and you have always had a longing to be free in me and to find my path."

"When you left the road on a wrong signal, you sought my GPS and I was there directing you, opening the way of life and blessings. People along the way looked happy and joyous, and you looked back and they had completely taken the wrong turn. You loved me and them enough to pray."

"Seek me with all of your heart. In my word first; in conversation with me; in stillness, listening; letting me express in words, in art, in song and in dance: myself in you, the hope of glory. You abide under the shadow of my wings. They are feathers. They are soft. I bundle you in my love that never changes or grows old or is offended. I will always draw you by my Spirit because you love me. I will keep you in perfect peace today, and always, as you keep your mind on me."

Day 6: Words from God to this young generation

"My beloved children, I, your heavenly Father have brought you through the fire of adversity and now you are in a high place and you can see the green pastures below and the living water flowing in the streams below. Keep close to this peace and joy that only comes as you drink from the fountain of life. In that fountain is my holy word that springs forth in your soul as you read and meditate on it. There are lots of places to read, but I will direct your reading if you wait before me. I have strengthened you in your inner being and I have given you beauty for ashes and a song of joy in a dry land and you dance in the breeze in my Holy Spirit: free to love, free to forgive, free to hope and have deep joy that comes only from me inside of you. Dance, my children, sing and rejoice, as you are my beloved and I am well pleased with you. I will add more and more to you as you focus on me in every assignment and obey me. This day rejoice. All is well."

Day 7: Words from God to this young generation

"My beloved child, before you were in your mother's womb you belonged to me. I have plans for you for an abundant life. I have plans for the abundant life for all who seek me above themselves. You are to increase my kingdom. No one knows--not even you know--but day by day I will reveal this to you as you seek me with all of your heart and love me more than yourself or others. Love me first and your love will never fail. Your eyes have not seen, neither has your ears heard what plans I have for you, but the Holy Spirit will reveal it to you. I love you with an everlasting love. I feed you daily as you wait for me to fill you and you are like a well-watered garden that brings forth fruit that remains."

Day 8: Words from God to this young generation

"My dearest child, I love you. I love every cell of your body. See each cell washed in the blood of my Son to restore, to renew, and to keep you from disease and pain, to bring me glory in the beauty of holiness. I have called you since birth to be mine. I have given you to live in my presence and in my will, to be my light too and to make me happy as your Father. I know, love and am thankful for each step of your life. When you fell, you looked to me. When you were hurt, you let me heal you. When you did not know what to do, you trusted me. I have put you here in this place at this time. My timing is perfect. Because of my grace and the beauty of your love you will live forever with me. That is huge in my site. Embrace this truth with your whole being and great thanksgiving will flow from you in the difficulty of this moment that brings eternal joy and eternal life. Seek me and thank me together and you will always feel peace in the storms."

Day 9: Words from God to this young generation

"My precious one, I want you to see yourself as I see you. I created you to be the beauty of my holiness in spirit, in soul, and body. Just as my Spirit and love has removed any sin that you so easily entreated when your eyes were not stayed on me or your mind was in turmoil, searching for peace and truth; I can cleanse your body of sickness or disease. My word says in Psalm 103, "Bless the Lord, oh my soul and all that is within me bless his holy name (forget not his benefits), who has forgiven all my sins, healed all of my diseases, kept me from sudden destruction and poured loving kindness and tender mercies upon me. Bless the Lord, oh my soul." Jesus is your joy and peace and health. Man has chiseled health away from the wholeness of your body. I make you whole. Let me heal you."

Day 10: Words from God to this young generation

"My precious jewel that sparkles in the sun of righteousness, I love you and keep you as the apple of my eye. Walk listening for my voice behind your ear and hear me say, "Go this way, do this or that." I have never failed you when you asked me. Sometimes it is quick, sometimes long to you. Rejoice with great joy today. See yourself free, climbing trees, dancing in the snow, running with whole knees. You are whole and free. Pain has no place in your heart to run over into your body. I have borne your grief and carried your sorrow and your pain was my pain on the cross."

"My beloved, you do have a Father in heaven that loves you with a perfect love and a father on earth who loves you with all his heart, but his heart has turned into himself. Remember the story of Joseph. You love me with all your heart and soul and forgive with my forgiveness and receive my coat of many colors: your beauty of spirit, soul and body, and know and feel the manna of my love from heaven that satisfies. Only my love satisfies. Sometimes it comes through selfless human beings who love with my love, but from me it is always just receive it, and know my plans are bigger than your mind, bigger than your fears."

Day 12: Words from God to this young generation

"My precious one, today I will give you clear direction because you seek me and because you care about my thoughts and plans for your life. I will send down my love and care and teach you my ways as you live and move and shake this world of darkness, and bring great light by the gifts that I have given to you. Rejoice, as the gates of hell cannot prevail against the church. You are my church. My blood covers you and keeps you. My truth leads and guides you. My love keeps you one and in great joy, no matter what you see or hear. Seek me with all you heart and rejoice always in me."

Day 13: Words from God to this young generation

"My beloved child from birth, you are my precious one. You have my heart and my mind since you were born. I have plans for you that were there before you entered this world. Watch and see. Watch and see each day. Know me, your Father in Heaven. Let the big space between earth and heaven be closed by my presence in you, the hope of Glory. It is all very simple and very vast at the same time. My plan is perfect for you, as was my perfect plan to send my Son for your salvation and for filling you with my Spirit to guide you in this life and eternity. Know that you are loved and my hand is guiding you. Follow your peace: that is my signal to follow my plan for you. Follow your peace and know in a situation no matter what the world or those in the world say, Jesus, my Son, is in you and he always knows what to do."

Day 14: Words from God to this young generation

"My dearly beloved, you do not see yourself as I
see you. You see yourself as others see you. To
know me and to know who I am in you, spend time
in absolute silence and keep saying you enter
where I am by the blood of Jesus and I enter
where you are. Your heart is my mercy seat and
your body is my temple. My Spirit in heaven and
my Spirit in your temple are one, and all
accusations and all fear of man and what they
think and all words spoken in ignorance or in a
controlling spirit will disappear. You will not be
afraid of exposure because your vessel is washed
each day by my blood, my presence, and my word.
This washing is as important as your daily shower
to cleanse your body. Rejoice in me. I am the way,
the truth, and the life. Have mercy on those who
love you and have used their own mindsets for
your protection. You can say with Jesus, "Father
forgive them as they know not what they do," and
your forgiveness and my perfect love shed abroad
in your heart will set them free and you will be
free."

Day 15: Words from God to this young generation

"My precious one, I know you are weary and tired. I am standing right by your side and my Son by the power of my Holy Spirit is in you. You will not give in by default. Just call on me. Say "Jesus", and wait. And I will bring a surge of my energy, my life and my hope to you in this dark hour. Rejoice, even if your mind, soul and spirit cry out. In doing this you release my hand in the situation because you are showing that you trust me to do the best I can for all. I am sending mercy drops from heaven down on all your love. Embrace me in this present darkness, and my light, my glory and my strength will take you through in peace."

Day 16: Words from God to this young generation

"My precious one, the root of bitterness that has grown in you since childhood has been destroyed by my light and my truth. That which was hidden in darkness that you knew in your spirit was wrong (but had no recourse over) is gone and you do not have to be bitter or angry anymore. You are free in my perfect love. I ask you to be so free that you can love as you walk in the freedom of the Spirit. And you never have to be subservient to another's spirit of control or manipulation. You are in me. I am in you and you will know what to do. Love, I will take care of the rest. Have mercy and I will always show you mercy. Judge not and you will never be judged. I am so grateful that you chose to run the race and not turn back or be stopped to die along the way. Live, live, live abundantly. I am your life."

My child, I am the Bright and Morning Star. My mercy is new every morning. This night rest in me as you tuck yourself in with the Lord's Prayer and the 23rd Psalm. Let the angels minister my Spirit to you during the night. I made your body to rest in me and face the morning with mercy. It is up to you the rest of the day to discipline your mind and heart to be stayed on me. There will be blizzards of bad news, confusion and sad tales. There are many things you cannot even do one thing about so cast them quickly to me, believing I care and that I will answer. Just cast and know. Others you hold in your hand and keep them before me because they can't bring themselves. At that moment I carry you in love, joy and peace, and you are safe from the enemy. Carry those you love, as they are not heavy if you are both in my arms."

Day 18: Words from God to this young generation

"My beloved, I AM with your generation. I am calling you from the backside of the desert just like I called Moses. You say, "Not me; I don't like to speak," but I say, "I AM." Answer my call and I will show you ways to let this generation go from the bondage of sin to the deliverance from Pharaoh and the Egyptian gods that still rule in the kingdom of this earth. I have placed dreams in your head. I have prepared you for excellence, but the only way to fulfill those dreams is to daily ask for my wisdom and forsake all and follow that wisdom. I am joy. I am peace. I am life and I am light. I am the way, the truth and the life. To know me is to know freedom and fulfillment, as I play upon the instruments of your lives. Let me increase the kingdoms of this world to the kingdom of my Son through your oneness and faithfulness and my wisdom."

Day 19: Words from God to this young generation

"My beloved and princess of Jesus, you know in your heart that you have been chosen by me your Father in heaven to walk with me. What you are to do is not written in a contract or a plan that you can see. It is a day by day walk of surrender and intimacy. It is bathing in my word and my sounds in your life. I AM. This time of separation from the days and the family of your youth will make you stronger. And if you keep praying for those you love and are daily blessing them, and believing for your destiny and theirs you will reap a deep peace. I am purifying your motives, your thoughts and your life for my Glory. Don't kick against the pricks. Walk with me in the joy of salvation, remembering my faithfulness. I love you and I have great plans for you in my kingdom on earth that will increase. And my peace will increase. It is my zeal in you that increases this kingdom wherever you are. I love you and I am with you always. I made you and will keep you in perfect peace when your mind is stayed on me."

Notes

Made in the USA
Columbia, SC
02 July 2024

37856075R00037